FAST LANE

First published in 2008
by Franklin Watts

Text © Martin Glynn and Deborah Smith 2008
Illustrations © Jade 2008
Cover design by Peter Scoulding

Franklin Watts
338 Euston Road
London NW1 3BH

Franklin Watts Australia
Level 17/207 Kent Street
Sydney, NSW 2000

A CIP catalogue record for this book
is available from the British Library.

ISBN: 978 0 7496 7712 1

Printed in Great Britain

Franklin Watts is a division of Hachette Children's Books,
an Hachette Livre UK company.
www.hachettelivre.co.uk

Blood Bond

Spike T. Adams

Illustrated by Jade

FRANKLIN WATTS
LONDON•SYDNEY

Chapter 1

I'm with Troy at the Endz Crew base.

"Yo! Troy!" JT calls.

JT runs the crew.

Troy walks over there.

They touch fists.

I wanna join the Endz Crew.

Like my big brother Troy.

Want it more than anything.

But it's down to JT.

As we leave, Otis walks by.

On his way home.

"Yo! College Boy!" Poppa J calls.

"Going home to ya momma?" Ruffneck asks.

Some of the crew laugh.

But Otis blanks them.

"Ya think ya too stush!" Poppa J goes on.

"But ya ain't jack!" finishes Ruffneck.

Otis just keeps on walking.

Otis is my other brother.

Mine and Troy's.

Otis ain't a team player.

Just wants his guitar and his books.

We don't talk too much.

Troy is the man to me.

I don't like how the crew pack Otis.

But I swallow it.

Coz Otis wants nothing to do with the Endz.

And that pisses off JT and the others.

JT eyeballs Troy.

"Ya need to deal with ya brother Otis," he says.

"He needs to show Endz some respect!"

Troy nods. "Yo, blood! Don't stress. I'll deal with it," he says.

"Ya know that!" JT goes on.

They touch fists.

But *I* feel stress.

Coz I don't know what Troy's gonna do.

What can he do?

He can't change Otis.

Only Otis can do that.

Chapter 2

Next morning, Mum is on at me again.

Cussing me for hanging with the Endz.

"Why you have to waste your life?"

"Looking for trouble, like Troy!"

"Why can't you be like Otis?"

I don't wanna hear it.

I miss Dad – he ain't around no more.

But when I'm with the Endz...

...I don't need him.

Mum cuts her eye at me and goes out.

Now Mum's gone, Troy comes in.

Mum and him row a lot.

Troy sees Otis sitting there.

Kisses his teeth.

"Troy, why ya stressing me?" Otis asks.

"Coz ya getting *me* stress, bro!" Troy tells him.

"The Crew ain't happy with ya."

Otis shrugs. "It ain't my crew, bro," he says.

Troy looks well vexed now.

Looks like things are gonna kick off.

Then the doorbell goes.

Otis gets up to see who it is.

Milly comes in.

"Hey Girl! What's gwaanin?" Paula says.

"What's she doing here?" Troy snaps.

"Her brother leads the Viper Crew!"

"She's my friend — and she's here to see me!"
Paula snaps back.

Milly glares at Troy and sits down.

"And I ain't in any gang!" Milly says.

Troy kisses his teeth again.

"Ya ain't got a clue!" he says.

"Ya blood leads the Viper Crew — that makes
ya Viper Crew."

And he storms out.

Paula and Milly both shrug.

And then Milly turns to Otis.

She gives him a big smile.

"How's ya band coming on?" she asks.

"OK," he tells her. "First gig next month."

"Safe! I'll be there!" she says.

Otis looks well pleased.

Paula pulls on her coat. "Let's hit the shops, Miss M."

At the door, Milly turns to Otis.

Flashes that smile again.

"We'll be at Dutchie's later," she says.

"See ya there?"

Otis smiles back.

"Maybe," he says.

Milly shuts the door.

I look at Otis. Shocked.

"Bro! Ya can't mess with her!" I tell him.

"Ya wanna piss the Vipers off as well as the Endz?"

"Ya can't tell me who to hang with," Otis says.

"If I wanna check Milly, I will."

I shake my head.

"Ya gonna get merked!" I warn him.

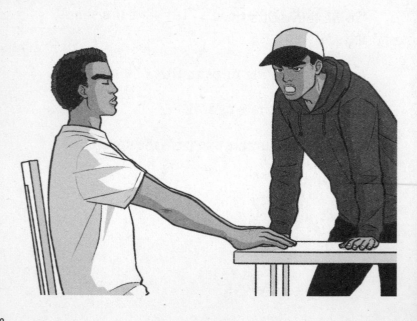

Troy comes back in.

Ready to meet the Crew.

"Let's go," he says to me.

I grab my jacket.

"Wanna come?" I ask Otis.

One last try.

Otis holds up his book.

Troy kisses his teeth.

So we leave Otis there.

Chapter 3

We go down to the pool hall.

Ruffneck lets me play him.

Poppa J buys me a drink.

Running with the Endz is da bomb!

Otis is a fool.

It's way better than studying.

Carlton shouts at Troy.

"Yo! You owe me, blood!"

Troy is laughing — dunno what he's done.

Carlton and him start play fighting.

Some people leave. Scared.

Endz just keep on playing.

Next day, I hear Paula on her mobile.

Teasing Milly.

"Otis never showed up at Dutchie's before!" she says.

"Milly, I can tell — he likes ya flex!"

So Otis went to see Milly last night...

I go up to her.

"Paula, what ya doing?" I say.

"Milly is linked to Viper Crew!"

Paula kisses her teeth at me.

Pushes me out.

Slams her bedroom door.

"Keep ya nose out!" she yells.

I shake my head.

"Ya heard what Troy said!" I yell back.

Chapter 4

A few days later, I'm walking down North Street.

There's a couple on the other side.

In a clinch.

I stop in my tracks. Shocked.

Coz it's Otis and Milly.

I watch them go into Dutchie's.

Gotta go over there.

Tell them.

They're messing with fire!

I cross the road.

But just then, the Viper Crew roll up.

Shit!

What's Ab gonna do when he sees his sister?

In Dutchie's.

With an Endz blood...

I follow them.

Stay just outside the door.

Ab clocks them in about two seconds flat.

He goes over.

Looks Otis up and down.

Kisses his teeth.

Then he turns to Milly.

"What ya doing with him?" he snaps.

"We're just gonna eat, that's all!" Milly snaps back.

"No ya ain't," Ab tells her.

"Get rid of the Endz blood."

His voice is cold as ice.

"Or I will..."

"We don't want any trouble, man," Otis tells Ab.

Ab gets right in Otis's face. "Well ya got it."

One of the Viper Crew cocks his fingers.

Aims it at Otis. Like a gun.

He laughs.

Milly pulls Otis away.

They don't see me as they rush past.

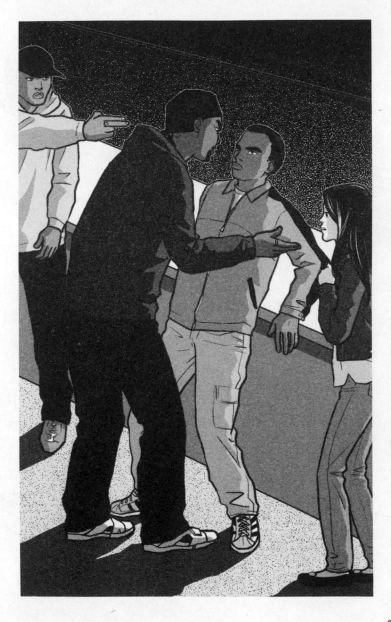

I hurry after them — grab Otis's arm.

"Bwoy! The two of ya must be mad!" I shout.

"Ya gotta stop this!"

Otis shakes me off.

I'm shocked at how strong he is.

I don't think of Otis as strong.

"Leave us alone, Devon," he says.

I watch them walk up the street.

Then I phone Troy.

Tell him what's gone down.

"Link JT — show him the runnings!" Troy tells me.

He is well vexed.

Chapter 5

I get over to JT's.

Tell the crew what went down at Dutchie's.

"Otis got dissed for being linked to Endz!" shouts Troy.

"Any way ya look at it, Vipers dissed us!"

"Da beef is on," says Ruffneck.

"And it ain't gonna be no play fight," Poppa J says.

JT turns to me. "Yo! Devon, ya done good," he says.

"Time ya rolled with us."

JT comes over. We touch fists.

It feels good.

I'm one of the crew.

Troy's mobile rings.

He flicks it open.

"Razor," he tells us.

"Yo!"

Razor talks. Troy listens.

Looking at Troy's face, the news ain't good.

He flicks the phone off.

"Vipers shot Otis," he says.

Troy looks at me. "We gotta get to the hospital."

I follow him out. Scared.

Troy looks scared too.

All those family rows —

— they don't matter any more.

Otis. Our brother. Our blood.

Shot.

We get to the hospital.

Rush up to the desk.

Tell them we're looking for Otis.

A nurse takes us to a bed.

Curtains all around it.

We go in. Mum is there.

And Paula, and Milly.

Otis is still. Like a statue.

Mum looks up.

"He's dead," she says.

"One of my babies — dead."

Me and Troy sit down.

Like we're in a trance.

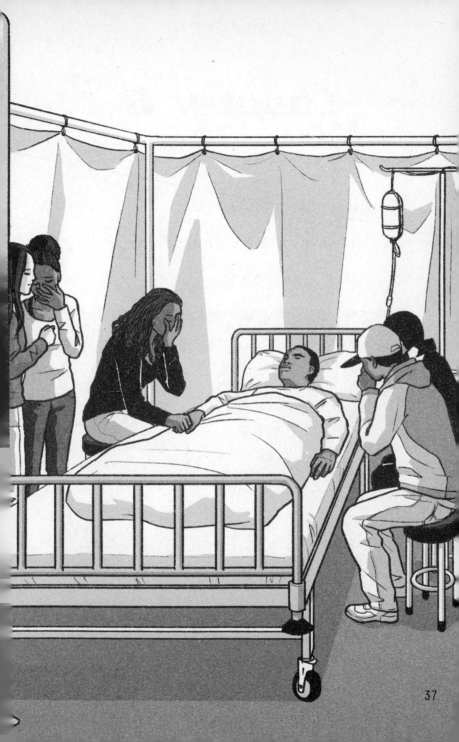

37

Chapter 6

It's two in the morning.

Mum kisses Otis for the last time.

She wails — like she is dying herself.

Paula and Milly sob next to her.

Milly's dad is outside.

She runs to him.

He takes her off in his car.

We all get into Troy's car.

Drive home along the dark streets.

No one speaks.

But my head is full of stuff.

Like, what happens now?

Next day, flowers and cards start arriving.

It makes Mum and Paula cry more.

Everyone is talking.

But not to the police.

I just wanna stay home.

Think about Otis.

But Troy comes and goes.

Like he can't keep still.

I hear him on his mobile.

"Even if Ab didn't shoot, he ordered it."

They're talking revenge.

We have dinner.

But no one eats much.

"I'm going to see Milly," Paula says.

She looks Troy in the eye.

For once, he says nothing.

Guess he doesn't wanna upset Mum.

Troy gets ready to link with the Endz.

"Ya coming?" he asks me.

I shake my head.

I wanna stay home.

To think about Otis.

I watch Troy walk down the road.

See him shake his head.

Punch a wall.

He don't say — but he's feeling the grief.

Mum gets out photos.

Ones from years ago.

When Troy and Otis and me and Paula were little.

Otis is in all of them.

She cries again.

I feel my eyes burn with tears.

45

And then a gun shot rings out down the street.

Mum clutches her heart.

"Who this time?" she says.

I run down the street. Fast as I can.

The sirens scream ahead of me.

Police and ambulance.

Chapter 7

There's a crowd outside Dutchie's.

I run over there, breathing hard.

Chest bursting.

"I think he's dead!" a woman says.

A policeman is putting tape across the doors.

I slip inside before he sees me.

First thing I see is Paula, crying.

With a policewoman.

Troy. It must be Troy.

I shake my head.

Mum. Two sons dead.

She's gonna die of a broken heart.

Then I see the medics.

Three of them, leaning over Troy.

Putting in needles.

Jolting his heart.

Thud.

Thud.

My own heart feels the shock.

Paula sees me.

She comes running over.

Shaking and crying.

"Ya see it happen?" I ask.

She nods.

"I... never seen... anyone... shot before..."

"Who pulled the trigger?"

I have to know.

Paula can't tell me.

Just starts sobbing again.

Then the medics stand up.

Shake their heads.

I go over.

Slowly.

To see Troy.

But when I get up close, I gasp.

Coz it's not Troy down there on the floor.

Dead.

It's Ab...

The policewoman comes past.

Milly is with her now...

"So where did you get the gun, Milly?" she asks.

Milly shot Ab?

"From Ab's car. It's his gun," Milly tells her.

She looks down at her brother's dead body.

"Ya gun took Otis," she says.

"Now it's taken you. End of."

Chapter 8

At Otis's funeral, Mum speaks out.

"All this killing — all this fear!

No winners — just losers.

Like my Otis..." she sobs.

"When will this end?"

For me, it ends here.

For Otis.

Running around with guns —

— I don't want it.

I've seen the blood.

Felt the pain.

It's not too late for me — to get out.

Go to college — have a different life.

Learn to play Otis's guitar.

Keep him with me.

Troy?

He still don't get it.

But maybe it's too late for him...

Amir wants to play for the school football team — the Hill Street Hawks.

The Stone Crew have other ideas.

But Amir won't be pushed around...

978 0 7496 7715 2

More titles by Spike T. Adams:

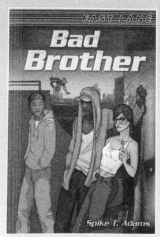

978 0 7496 7713 8

978 0 7496 7714 5